This book is a unique cultural critique that shows various dimensions of what's going on in the world. It is a chronicle of what I have experienced and what the truth is for me. My intention is not to tell others that their beliefs are wrong or less important. My aim is to create an exchange of open dialog and to stimulate positive change. Some of the subjects that I spotlight are politics, economics, spirituality, religion, environmental issues, job loss and false images and the media. It may seem like these are separate issues, but they are intricately connected. This book took about twenty years to compose and is a culmination of almost two decades of study on some painful subjects. Still, it was a catharsis to write. Though these topics are controversial, I'm just trying to give a realistic portrayal of what's happening in the world through my eyes.

CONNECT THE DOTS

C. M. CROCE

Published by
Human Error Publishing
www.humanerrorpublishing.com
paul@humanerrorpublishing.com

Copyright © 2016
by
Human Error Publishing
&
C. M. Croce

All Rights Reserved

ISBN: 978-0-9833344-7-7

Front Cover: C. M. Croce

Back Cover by:
Human Error Publishing
&
C. M. Croce

Human Error Publishing asks that no part of this publication be reproduced or transmitted in any form or by any means electronic or mechanical, including photocopy, recording or information storage or retrieval system without permission in writing from C. M. Croce and Human Error Publishing. The reasons for this are to help support the artist.

ACKNOWLEDGMENTS

To my dear family,
without your unconditional love
and support and the close connection
that we share, I could not
have accomplished all that I have.
Along with my family,
I would like to give special thanks
to the many kindred spirits
that I have been lucky enough
to meet on my life's journey,
including my many mentors,
who have taught me much.
There are not enough words
in the world to express
my love and gratitude.
Now to my esteemed readers,
settle in and then follow
in the direction of your dreams.
Express yourselves fully,
but avoid all extremes.

Table of Contents

AN INHERENT POWER	8
MEDITATION BRINGS REVELATION	9
A LIFE'S SONG	10
A SOUL CONNECTION	11
IN FULL VIEW	12
PHILOSOPHY	13
A LIGHT IN THE DARK	14
WINGS	15
AN ELEMENT OF TRUTH	16
DESTINY	17
LET'S LIVE FOR THE PLUNDER OF IT ALL	18
A MISPLACED PASSION	20
OPPRESSION REIGNS ON THE DARKEST DAYS	21
THE DEVASTATION TO CONSERVATION	23
A FOOLISH ENDEAVOR	24
DIVERSITY IS NOT OUR ENEMY	26
THE PATRICIAN'S POSITION	27
CORPORATE LEVIATHAN	28
NECESSITY	30
THE GDP IS NOT SUBSTANCE FREE	31
THE MALICE PHALLUS	32
WHO'S WHO IN THIS RICH WITCHES' BREW	34
ANOTHER SERIOUS SETBACK	36
AN EXTOLLED ERROR	37
EVOLVE OR DIE	38
PALATABLE POISON	41
A HEARTBREAK IS LIKE AN EARTHQUAKE	43
THE APPETITE OF THE ALMIGHTY PARASITE	44
MOTHER EARTH	45
THE PRODUCTION OF DESTRUCTION	47
YOU CANNOT CLEANSE A SIN	48
101 WORDS THAT SPELL HELL	50
TEN QUESTIONS ABOUT 9/11	51
THE POLLUTION-FREE ENERGY CONSPIRACY	52
THE LEANER, MEANER, GLOBAL FREE TRADE ARENA	54
TRAGEDY AND BETRAYAL	56

LITTLE HAS CHANGED	57
THE CAUSE	58
INVENTORS AT THE CENTER OF THE CRIMINALLY INSANE	59
WHAT IS WRONG WITH THIS PICTURE	61
GLOBAL MANIFEST DESTINY	63
IMAGINE WHAT IT WOULD BE LIKE	66
WE BRING GOOD THINGS TO LIFE	68
THE MACHINIST'S PLIGHT	70
THE DECEITFUL ARTIST OF ALLOCUTION	72
THE WELCH WAY	75
TOO MANY UNLUCKY NUMBERS	78
A DISEMBODIED-VOICE DREAM	79
THE TERRAIN HAS CHANGED	81
OUTRAGEOUS ACCOLADES OF THE POACHER'S TRADE	82
THE HIDDEN FEE	83
A FALLING STAR	85
THE ME GENERATION	86
MERCURY IN RETROGRADE	87
THE DEN OF AMERICA'S POLITICAL MIDDLEMEN	89
THE PRESENT STATE	91
READ MY LIPS I NEVER LIE	92
THE PROBLEM WITH IMPERFECT POWER	95
QUESTIONING COMPETITION WITHIN THE COLONY	96
A UNIQUE CULTURAL CRITIQUE	97
A FALSE IMAGE	98
THE ANIMA AND THE ANIMUS	99
GUARANTEED AUTHENTIC	100
ARE WE AUTHENTIC OR NOT	101
THE BLEEDING HEART	102
A LOSS OF SPIRIT	103
THE DISCOVERY OF FULL RECOVERY	104
SUFFERING STANDING STILL	106
A BEE ANALOGY	107
A VESTED INTEREST	109
THE REIGN OF CAIN	111
THE WAR AGAINST THE WORLD	112
THE INDIGENOUS, THE ENDANGERED, THE LINK TO THE EXTINCT	113
ONCE THE BLOOD IS WASHED AWAY	114

LIFE REDUCED TO A DOLLAR	115
FOOD FOR THOUGHT	116
THE CONVEYOR BELT / THE SHOOT	117
NOBODY IS 100% POSITIVE	119
JOINED OPPOSITION	120
FAITH IN THE FACE OF FEAR	121
GOD IS LOVE	122
I AM A LEXIGRAM	125
LOVE DOES NOT HATE OR DISCRIMINATE	126
MIND STATES	127
IN OUR HEARTS	128
LOVE IS AT THE CENTER OF OUR BEING	129
CARING, SHARING AND EQUALITY	130
A PIECE OF THE PUZZLE	131
A DEDICATION	133
NOTES	134

AN INHERENT POWER

THAT WAS PREDESTINED TO FLOWER

I remember the seed
that planted the deep need to proceed.
In a dream my studies began
of me and my relationship
with the whole of man.
It was my grandfather's words that I heard.
A line he had used before.
It was a hook to take an inner look.
It opened the door to what was in store.

MEDITATION BRINGS REVELATION

No strings attached;
completely set free.
A mind cleared,
spacious and empty.
Enter creative energy.
Quietly, we converse
with the universe.

A LIFE'S SONG

I am one fine line of the divine.
A single chord of the Lord,
a key vibration of energy,
and I give glory to the powers that be
that are playing with me in harmony.

A SOUL CONNECTION

A TWIST OF FATE / LIFE IS REALLY A FIGURE EIGHT

My beloved home is on the Mohawk Trail
where the setting of Autumn is beautiful,
yet sad and solemn.
I am sure that I have stood here before
and as I stand on this sacred ground,
I feel a feeling that is so profound.
I am now of the genetic race
that mowed my people down.
There is a veil between the past
and the present that is so thin,
and if we go within,
we will not only know where we are,
we will also get a sense of where we've been.
Cell memory, our soul, it remembers it all.
It even remembers what we don't recall.
It remembers the love; it remembers the connection.
It remembers the loss and the lack of protection.
It remembers an attack from lifetimes back,
and it even remembers how we fought back.
Now my soul is calling and I have to call it back.
Wisdom is intuition and it is our soul mission to listen!

IN FULL VIEW

INTEGRITY IN POETRY AND PHILOSOPHY

If a philosophy is a game, a show, or a shell,
it is not worth wasting your breath to tell.
Once we focus on being a philosophical poet,
life changes as we know it.
First we grope to understand
and when we do, it must ring true.
The discomfort that a lie or an error can cause
magnifies our weaknesses and our flaws.
It is hard to discard the easy way out,
because it is unpleasant work facing our doubt.
We cannot just leave it where it lies.
When it comes to the truth there is no compromise.
We are different. We no longer belong.
How dare we point out what is right and wrong?
We are scorned, we are shunned;
we are offensive to those we've stunned.
For the truth hurts, the truth exposes;
the truth opens what ignorance closes.

PHILOSOPHY

IS A LOVE OF SOPHIA

From the truth you hold, honesty is told.
Poetry arising from an unjust trend.
Universal messages to sculpt and blend.
You're my trusted companion;
my faithful friend,
I grieve when I leave and rejoice
at the slightest presence of your voice.

A LIGHT IN THE DARK

The persistent act
of pecking out of the shell
delivers water from the deepest well.
I was given this gift;
I helped it to grow.
This is the meaning of
"you reap what you sow."
Nobody "lights a candle"
and then "puts it under a bowl."
And you never gave us a candle
that was too hot to hold.
You gave us free will
to develop our God-given skills
not only to put food on the table,
but to be ready, willing and able
to be a bright spark
that lightens up even the deepest,
most depressed regions of the dark.
Is this what we call a work of art,
or a purposeful, but often painful,
opening of our heart?

WINGS

OF A DEVELOPING FLEDGLING

Fluttering
under the radar,
emitting
an occasional
flash of light,
mustering
the strength
to finally
take flight.

AN ELEMENT OF TRUTH

Have you heard the latest word?
There's magic in our national bird.
There's only one catch:
To be number one, you have to eat it.
The Bald Eagle, but that's illegal?
Have no fear,
we have greed working for us here.
Before you can say "taboo,"
we'll make it legal to eat Bald Eagle stew.

DESTINY

Put me on the path
that you have planned for me
and weaken my resistance,
so I will go willingly.
For life is no accident;
each life is your plan,
but whether or not
one fulfills his or her destiny
is dependent upon
the size of the strength
of each woman, child and man.
Now what will it take
for us to understand
that strength is measured
by the size of the heart,
not the power of the hand?
Now all too often,
yes much too often,
it is the most powerful man
who takes the weakest stand.

LET'S LIVE FOR THE PLUNDER OF IT ALL

It is best to start at the beginning
and pray we are not near the end.
Throughout our American history,
America has made many, many enemies
and hopefully for our sake a few true friends.
Now America cannot distance itself
from the wealth and land it has gained,
no more than it can distance itself
from how they were attained.
From the onset of time,
America's excessive need for expansion
has led ambitious men
to commit some of the most unforgivable,
inexcusable crimes:
such as the merciless slaughter
of the American Indians in a betrayal of tears
and taking the land that was rightfully theirs;
and the crazy, lazy labor plan
of seizing the African people from their homeland,
and the justification for this dehumanization
was they needed slaves to work their plantations;
and the unjust gain of 55% of Mexico's terrain.
This border that they cross is really land that they lost.
And also the sickening institution
of exploiting our immigrant ancestors,
who built this country during the industrial revolution.
Now it seems as if it is thought
everyone has forgiven and forgot.
Someone's smoking way too much pot.
Other than greed,
there is sure to be some kind of addiction
the present people in power have got.
So much time has passed and so much has changed,
but the mindset with which America rules
has remained the same.
Yet, there is still a big, dangerous difference
between now and then,
because today America is ruled

by a few powerful, unpatriotic, disloyal men.
Not even the welfare of America itself
is first and foremost on their minds.
All they can think about
is wallowing in the wealth
and rolling in the dough;
shareholder loyalty is all that they know.
They have regressed to the point
where they have no real loyalty
to their communities,
or even to their own country.
They have pushed the truth
and American pride aside
and are now taking
each and every one of us
on a reckless "Manifest Destiny" ride.
It has been said on many
memorable occasions
that history repeats itself.
Well, those old southern boys are back.
They are now in power
and they've put their slave trade
agenda back on track,
only this time it is they themselves
who are fleeing from our American site.
They have somehow managed
to free themselves from all the laws
that many a brave worker has won
in many a bloody fight.
The American people
need to open their eyes
to see this all too painful reality.
Boundless global free trade
has given back to the rich man
what was once taken away.
It is what he has longed for.
It is what he has craved.
He has somehow managed
to make foreign workers
his new poverty wage slaves.

A MISPLACED PASSION

Take heed from Icarus,
who flew too close to the sun
and became just another lost loved one.
Whether it is fortune or fame,
a Saddam Hussein,
heroin or cocaine,
the end result is the same.
So much suffering
on a meaningless cross,
and unlike your Savior,
what a complete and utter loss.

OPPRESSION REIGNS ON THE DARKEST DAYS

The powerful man has used his upper hand
to climb the ladder of success,
and all it takes is signing
to find the successful silver lining.
Now from where many an elite man stands,
the world is at his feet,
and he is now reigning down oppression
on those who have no retreat.
It is true; the pen is mightier than the sword
and with it wealth is their reward.
Now their exploited faces are right there
and the proof of their existence
has been kept concealed,
and it is only revealed
in what we buy, sell, eat and wear.
And the greedy governments,
who have supported
and laid down the ground work for this,
can't be taken off the hook,
just because they've stuck their heads
in the sand and have refused to look.
Being children of God,
is it not our God-given right
to know that the food we put in our mouths,
the clothes that we put on our backs,
the shoes that we put on our feet,
and every other luxury
that brings bodily comfort
to ourselves and our children
are not being brought to us
at the expense of others?
Was it not outrage
and the fear of a boycott
that brought us (Dolphin Safe) labels
on our tuna fish cans?
Are not people as valuable as dolphins?
Should we not be outraged,

and should we not demand
that products are brought to us
with genuine labels:
Made by Unexploited Hands?
Then maybe someday soon,
hope and nourishment will bloom
from all we consume.

THE DEVASTATION TO CONSERVATION

CAUSED BY GAS AND OIL EXPLORATION

Seismic and sonar testing:
It's not as innocent
as they make it sound,
and it's one of the reasons
that whales and dolphins
are running themselves aground.
One hundred thousand times [1]
louder than a jet engine's roar,
they're killing and injuring
our sea creatures,
and the reverberations are felt
deep beneath the ocean floor.
Sadly, what eyewitnesses
have come across
is habitat and hearing loss,
and brain hemorrhages,
mass confusion and chaos.
Every ten seconds,
twenty-four hours a day, [1]
they're assaulting the senses
and anything that gets in their way.
In their quest for success,
you cannot count on one hand
all that offshore drilling is killing.
Even as we speak,
both life and limb are being threatened
from the east and from the west,
and it all begins with a seismic test!

A FOOLISH ENDEAVOR

FOR EXTINCTION IS FOREVER

The dead sea is a poignant analogy!
Too many waterways are being appraised
and are in peril of becoming sterile.
Now our warming seas are critically diseased
and our animal kingdom is in turmoil,
and still they won't stop
until they have spilled every last drop
of gas, blood and oil.
There are red lights and there are green lights
and to proceed with caution is in between,
but the only color they want to see is green.
As an aggressor, they apply pressure
and draw hostility towards anyone who tries to resist,
and since large amounts of money are involved,
it can get downright dangerous.
Just ask the noble protectors
of the Virunga National Park,
who have been relentlessly besieged
by murderous butchers, poachers and thieves,
including a hostile army of heavily armed rebels
who have the same agenda as SOCO International,
because this British oil company
has proven itself to be a big spender. (2)
From **volcanic** Lake Edward
in the Virunga National Park,
to all the exploited gulfs from coast to coast,
how can we allow the energy industry
to cause such mayhem
and make nature's beauty a mere ghost?
Many of us have never seen
most of the animals out in the wild,
but still we know that they are there,
and it is painful to acknowledge
that they are about to disappear.
Will the majestic mountain gorillas
of Virunga be no more,

only to be spoken of in obscure folklore?
Will our Earth's most endangered species
become a dimming, distant memory,
only to be observed in a tank or in a cage
or perceived as a lonely picture on a page?
What a sad day it will be
when the only jungle that is left
beneath their feet is concrete.
Now there is a motive to their madness
that is causing us great sadness.
Once they destroy all that is endangered,
it need not be protected anymore.
Then they are free to explore
and mightily profit
from all that life once stood for.
There is a vast contrast
between those who value life
and those who treat it like trash,
to be used and discarded
and then regarded
as nothing more than a thing of the past.
To them, nothing is sacred
and they are leaving no stone unturned,
and they are pushing everything,
including our precious planet,
to the point of no return.
What good is money in the bank,
when there's nothing left to save?
What good is money in the end,
when our Earth becomes a lifeless grave?

DIVERSITY IS NOT OUR ENEMY

AND NEITHER IS UNITY

Noah's Ark is a symbolic stamp mark of diversity,
a seal of approval of how the Earth is supposed to be.
Now if modern man had to choose what to bring,
would he still include the same two of everything?
It is highly unlikely, and he would probably hoard
what he did decide to bring on board.

THE PATRICIAN'S POSITION

IN THIS DOOMSDAY POWER PLAY

Acquisition is a condition
where there are haves
and have-nots
and unfortunately the haves
are calling all the shots.
And they are so selfish,
spoiled rotten and immature,
and they look down upon
and belittle the needy,
the compassionate and the poor,
because they are blinded
by their delusions
of superiority and grandeur.
What other explanation
could be given
as to why they are killing
everything that is living,
and it just might explain
why they don't feel
anyone else's pain?

CORPORATE LEVIATHAN

IS DIMMING THE HORIZON

The locks on Pandora's box
were picked with precision and skill
by a drug addict using an unorthodox drill.
Yes, with their pipes and their lines,
they are the most dangerous
drug addicts of all times!
The head honcho of Halliburton,
and war profiteer
and two-time Vice President
of the United States,
whined about having to keep up
with our fuel-driven, consumer demands.
Yet, he has no intentions
of letting renewable energy
take this job from his hands.
With a finger in the dyke
and a massive pole in the hole,
there's no denying
that these people are out of control.
They're poisoning our planet;
they're deadening our seas,
and they're paying our government
percentage rate royalty fees.
Everyone knows
that oil and water don't mix,
and that offshore drilling
causes catastrophic oil slicks,
but that doesn't seem to upset
this hell-bent one percent.
Even after the Deepwater Horizon
botch and blunder,
where eleven workers died
and the oil rig went under
and the floodgates of hell
were broken open,
BP and the energy industry

had absolutely no remedy
and no remorse,
and they have no intentions
of changing their deadly course.
They are killers
on an apocalyptic scale,
and they're hiding their faces
behind a corporate veil.
They're the villain
and they're free
to do whatever they please,
and before long
they are going to bring
all of us to our knees.
They're a lawbreaker!
They're a lawmaker!
They're the belly of the beast!
They're our worst nightmare!
They are the mortal enemy of peace!

NECESSITY

IS THE MOTHER OF INVENTION

Leave the people hungry
for money and jobs,
and they will do
just about anything you want.
Anything you need
to satisfy your ghoulish greed
can be done,
even to the detriment
of everyone.
You are in line
with the energy industry
that gives light,
and are like an eclipse
that brings on the darkest night.
For you, many have given up
their hopes and dreams
and gone to their graves
mournfully beset with regret.
You have less than a century to live,
and you are taking way more
than you give.
When will you learn?
When much is given,
much is expected in return.

THE GDP IS NOT SUBSTANCE FREE

AND NEITHER ARE WE

Weapons, liquor, tobacco and pot,
gambling, drugs, illegal or not,
are some of the most
valuable commodities we've got.
Even the act of sodomy
is feeding our seedy, greedy economy.

THE MALICE PHALLUS

TO RAISE CAIN IS TO KILL
THE FREE WILL OF ABEL

Hydraulic drilling for oil and natural gas
is fracking our planet up the A$$.
First our government was hijacked.
Then they exempted themselves
from the Clean Water Act!
President George W. Bush gave
Cheney, and company a free pass
to fracture and poison our planet
with no questions asked.
What a diluted form of democracy,
when you can stir things up
and then let them brew,
poison people's water supplies
and leave them knowing
that there is nothing that they can do.
How could this happen?
How could this be?
How could the energy industry
have been allowed
to bypass our laws of democracy?
They stacked the deck,
so no one has the power
to keep them in check.
Again and again,
they have stacked the table
in favor of Cain, but not *Able*.
They grow disease, death and woe,
but have exempted themselves
from the proverb
"You reap what you sow."
Ignorance reigns supreme
when taken to the extreme.
It is said that the eyes
are the windows to the soul.
What darkness corrupted these beings

and obstructed their seeing,
so they see only themselves
winning a bountiful prize,
but fail to see the suffering,
and pollution, the ill retribution
that is triggered by their earth-shattering,
hydraulic fracturing solution?
Habitual home wreckers,
look what you have done!
If you and your families
were forced to dwell there,
how fast would you run?
Now pray that you don't
cause a **volcanic winter**
that blocks out the sun!

WHO'S WHO
IN THIS RICH WITCHES' BREW

Shell, ExxonMobil and BP
and another mortal enemy
of the Congo, SOCO,
and the list goes on and on.
They are the modern-day Genghis Khan
and with their power, size and speed,
they are the echelon of greed!
Their powerful influence
sets crushing wheels in motion,
and just because their actions
aren't as out in the open
as the tanks in Tiananmen Square,
they are still just as dangerous and cold,
and they certainly are
an ungodly sight to behold.
Now if we were to analyze and compare,
the industrial complex's activities
probably kill more in a day
than most terrorists will kill in a year.
They eliminate anything
that impedes their path.
Yet they are not held accountable
for the aftermath.
To them, litigation is a chess match
waiting to be won,
a court order
that allows them to kill at will
and then reload the smoking gun.
They systematically silence
our problem solvers and their solutions
and anyone that tries to reduce
their excessive pollution.
Who is more dangerous?
Who is more out of control?
Who deserves judgement
and incarceration more,
a two-time petty parolee

or these sick motherfrackers
that are destroying the world
just to get their score?
One thing is for sure,
as an industrial complex,
they are evil to the core
and if they continue to have their way,
we'll be extinct like the dinosaur.
Our scales of justice are dishonest
and the truth is in short supply,
because justifying corruption
is the code of conduct that they live by!
Now watch them shift their feet
and wink their eye
and pervert our politicians
with another diverted money supply.
Then once their political pawns
are in place,
they will defy all sensibilities
and in a complete breach of trust,
our disloyal lawmakers will slide in
riders, and open up loopholes,
and protect their Citizens United.
They could also call this,
conquer what you've divided.
There are those of us that disagree,
but we as a **united species**
can stop this doomsday power play.
What we need is a Roosevelt.
What we need is a New Deal,
but what we need most of all
are the balls to deflate these big wheels.
Now there are faces behind the corporate name.
Let us plaster them on the wall of shame.
Let us link their identity to each atrocity
and do away with this lack of transparency,
and all the laws that make these individuals
nameless and blameless,
and let us never forget
they are the real threat!

ANOTHER SERIOUS SETBACK

A Tribute to Nikola Tesla

In the early 1900s, Nikola Tesla,
the brilliant physicist, electrical engineer,
inventor, and also the man who brought us
AC "plug in" electricity declared,
Using the Earth's magnetic field,
he could electrify the world
with wireless electricity.
One would think that such a discovery
would be welcomed and embraced,
but no, because it upset
the monetary status quo,
it was erased with hardly a trace.
This energy problem, solving invention
was terminated by J. P. Morgan
prior to its full implementation.
His last words on the subject were,
"If anyone can draw on the power,
where do we put the meter?"
He then permanently pulled the plug.
This is a classic case
of an individual playing a leading role
in intentionally impeding
the progress of the whole.
Apparently, unless it can be piped,
metered and monopolized,
the full potential
of our Earth's renewable energy
will not be made available
for all of us to utilize.
We must now figure out
how to go about suspending
these unending setbacks.

AN EXTOLLED ERROR

IS A HOLY TERROR

All of us are attracted
to the good that we see,
because each and every one of us
wants to be happy.
And when we fix our aim
on the object of our desire,
the urge to orbit this object
gets higher and higher.
But if we are ignorant
and have a narrow-minded point of view,
an error will be seen as good
and it will be that which we pursue.
In addition, a college education
does not guarantee
a major degree in intelligence!

EVOLVE OR DIE

IS STARING US STRAIGHT IN THE EYE

We must cause this ignorant evil to pass
by peacefully marching en masse
in every city; in every town,
and we should not stop,
until the robber barons all back down.
For if they continue
with this desolate trend,
it is not a question of if;
it is a question of when.
Here they go again;
it's just a different blend.
Again, our energy officials misled us
and stated facts that were half true.
They asserted that natural gas
was cheaper and cleaner.
So we converted
and gas consumption grew.
If we only knew
what this would develop into:
a malice phallus, that drills and extracts
and is poisoning our Earth
and fracking her for all she is worth.
Billions of gallons of water
are being toxically treated.
We will die without water
and it's being poisoned and depleted.
Harmful emissions of methane
are being released into the air
with disastrous effects;
just ask the last polar bear.
This is no bridge!
For it goes from bad to worse
and threatens our existence on Earth.
We have been lied to;
we have been conned.
Now the day of reckoning has dawned.

Our country and our people
are being used and extorted,
so this explosive commodity
can be expanded and exported.
And where is it going?
To the highest bidder!
That's a bitter pill to swallow,
but what's even worse is what's to follow.
Kinder Morgan, an environmental menace,
and National Grid are pushing
the new pipeline proposals through.
They are springing into action
and are using price gouging as traction.
Supply and demand
should not be the law of the land,
but they are treating it as such;
a 37% price hike is way too much!
In economic terms,
our "life, liberty and pursuit of happiness"
are of no concern.
They are in the position of opposition,
so their compassionate component
is missing!
Now watch the drama unfold,
as these selfish lovers of gold
beat the war drum roll
over oil, natural gas and coal.
Our Earth's foundation is being shaken.
The energy industry has declared war
and our planet has weapons at her disposal,
including earthquakes, tsunamis and more.
They are not just digging up the dirt;
they're getting down to the nitty-gritty,
and what's being exposed
is anything but pretty.
How many states of emergency
have these tycoons made?
And why is it that it is the taxpayer
and not the profiteer who has paid?
They're sucking the Earth dry.

They're destroying our land.
What will it take
for us to draw a line in the tar sand?
Our forefathers finally revolted
over a tax on tea.
Yet this threat is being met
with a sheepish apathy.
It is not time to ask;
it is now time to demand
that our lawmakers abolish
these apocalyptic plans.
This is an "abomination
that causes desolation
standing where it does not belong…" [3]
And the time has come
for them to develop a green thumb!

PALATABLE POISON

AN UNWISE COMPROMISE

This modern day Medusa
is creating a systemic epidemic!
More and more unnatural,
less and less in control,
this tasty pervasive poison
is a ghoulish man's gold.
We are being forced to resort
to an unhealthy form of life support.
We are being made to comply
with a science experiment
that has gone horribly awry.
Take a look at our tampered-with
food supply.
It is filled with chemicals,
toxins and pesticides
and is engineered
and genetically modified,
and these arcane,
Frankenstein strains
that have been unleashed
in our fragile food chain
can no longer be contained.
We cannot even be sure
that our organics are pure,
because these fools
are changing the rules.
Stripped of its disguise,
our western diet
could be categorized
as a cancer-causing compromise.
With the most deceitful sound bites,
they secure their bottom line,
and the malignancy they cause
is anything but benign.
One wonders,
is it greed or calculation?

Is it all about the money
or decreasing the population?
Or perhaps it's the added appeal
that it's a two-for-one deal.
Now if we were to take this
in another direction,
we could definitely
link the connection
to Monsanto's
political puppet show
called "Quid Pro Quo,"
and the obvious, ill intentions
of the implementation
of state preemption.

A HEARTBREAK IS LIKE AN EARTHQUAKE

NO MORE CHILD'S PLAY

Youth seems like
a whisper away,
a time untouched
by entropy and decay.
The past didn't last;
now that's where
my loved ones lie.
Tears replaced the years;
how life-shattering
when a loved one dies,
never again to set foot
before our eyes.
It is said that time
heals all wounds,
but there are some
that we never
fully recover from.

THE APPETITE
OF THE ALMIGHTY PARASITE

Our Mother Earth
is being forcefully overfed
her fracking gross daily dose.
She is now being unjustly served
on a toxic-laden plate,
and what could possibly be the reason
for her most unfortunate fate?
The controversial reason is
that the rich and the powerful
have it made to order
from border to border.
We are all hosts to the most
powerful parasites on the planet.
They promise a symbiotic relationship,
but in turn, they're killing everything to live.
With their high-rise holes in the ozone
and their metastasized population control,
they think that they're the cream of the crop,
but they are no more than a flea.
A gnat, a tick, they are fracking sick;
they are pestilence to the highest degree.
And too late they'll learn
how little they know,
how small they are!
In light of their many transgressions,
let us close with one final question.
If the Creator delighted in the Earth's creation,
is sorrow felt at the sight of her devastation?

MOTHER EARTH

Earth is a celestial body
with energy coursing
through her veins.
She is the nurturing Mother
of all the life forms she sustains.
Her highest-born child
is both weak and wild
and is now somehow
responsible for her care.
This power-hungry son
could and should look after her,
but instead he pollutes and poisons
her body, water and air.
Now the relationship between them
is almost beyond repair.
Her son is well aware of his behavior
and all the selfish things that he has done,
but he justifies his actions by believing
that he is the most important one.
He has quite an insatiable appetite
and an immense amount of conceit,
and he thinks that if he has sex,
money and power
his life will be complete.
His current ideas and beliefs
are convoluted and contorted,
and his view of himself
and his view of the world
are one-sided and distorted.
He sees his Mother's
lungs as trees;
he cuts them down
and stifles the breeze
and the oil
beneath his Mother's soil.
It makes his blood boil.
Filled with pride,
prejudice and power,

he violently settles scores,
while his Mother Earth
wears the battle scars
of his never-ending wars.
He kills his brothers and sisters
and anything that swims,
crawls or flies.
Yet, he is still of the opinion
that he is civilized.
He finds his Mother's riches
most irresistible,
so he strips her of them all.
Will this contempt
that he feels for his Mother
eventually be his downfall?

THE PRODUCTION OF DESTRUCTION

Where did the weapons come from?
Where did they originate?
Who sold the weapons
to the hornet nests of hate?
Holistically, this world is one big family.
Yet, what have we done
with our advanced technology?
We've created an arms race.
We haven't got our values straight.
For these arms do not support or embrace.
No, these arms bomb and obliterate.
All because of blind ambition,
our Mother Earth is near critical condition
and what she needs now is a new physician.
For the old political order is in denial.
Yes, her old laissez-faire physicians
have all gone senile.
"United we stand, divided we fall"
was not meant for one nation;
it was meant for us all!

YOU CANNOT CLEANSE A SIN

BY SELLING KILLERS WEAPONS TO WIN

To combat Russia and Iran,
Ronald Reagan pumped weapons
into Iraq and Afghanistan.
Deals like this have always been done.
Many nations are doing this;
America's not the only one.
"The enemy of my enemy is my friend."
This is a dangerous trend that must end!
For the stakes are so much higher
than the threat of rapid gun fire.
For the weapons
that are now up for sale
cause devastation
on the most massive scale.
Albert Einstein expressed
something to this effect.
I do not know what weapons
will be used in World War III,
but it will be sticks and stones
that are used in World War IV.
One thing is for sure,
there is not much more
that our Mother Earth
and her inhabitants can endure.
This negative imbalance
to the greatest degree
is a cause for such urgency.
For modern man's
destructive ignorance is so great
and his thirst for Wisdom is so small,
and the amount of this disparity
reflects just how far
our living conditions will fall.
The powers that lead
are far from enlightened.
What they really are

is insecure and frightened,
and with the information
that they know, it is rightly so.
If we knew what they knew,
we'd be even more scared
and scarred than we already are!

101 WORDS THAT SPELL HELL

A WORLD IN CRISIS

There are high costs;
there are dire prices
for producing the likes
of Al Qaeda and ISIS.
This reign of pain
which cannot be contained
is a by-product
of self-centered capital gain.
We've armed them
and trained some;
now we must fight
for what is wrong
and what is right.
We have strengthened
and lengthened
their deadly reach
and have amplified
their power of speech.
Now we hear
the blaring battle cries
and see the tortured tears
of blood-stained innocent eyes.
Again, we face
this revolting campaign,
where the limbless untwist
the sacred from the profane.

TEN QUESTIONS ABOUT 9/11

Has one of our worst
nightmares just come true?
Are there evil monsters
living among me and you?
First there was World War I,
then World War II;
could this be the entry
into World War III?
Here we face
a new type of enemy
who has successfully
infiltrated our own country.
What lines got crossed
before the Twin Towers fell?
And what thoughts of heaven
could possibly lead to this living hell?
How in the name of religion
can such evil deeds be done?
How can thoughts of good
and acts of evil
be all rolled up into one?
9/11, religious zeal,
how can sadistic hatred
have a sacred appeal?
Tell us then, if God is Love
and Love does not hate or discriminate,
how can anyone
kill and maim
and then proclaim
that it was done
in the Lord's name?
One more question;
if Iraq were Rwanda
or a pile of rocks
with no oil
beneath her soil,
would our leaders
have liberated her?

THE POLLUTION FREE ENERGY CONSPIRACY

Many of the people in power
believe in the Bible's Revelation
and because of this belief,
they think the end is inevitable
and close at hand.
This must be why they lack vision.
This must be why they have devised
no real future energy plan.
They have the confidence and the skill
to fly to the moon and back.
They have the courage and the will
to destroy and hopefully rebuild oil-rich Iraq.
But it will be a cold day in hell
before these top oil cartels
will allow pollution-free energy
to surpass even the last remaining oil wells.
For they know, as long as they can hold us
over a barrel and rake us over the coal,
they possess the power
to keep us under their control.
How much more in research
and development would be done
if our government believed
the power of the sun
could successfully produce
a solar death-ray gun?
It is sad to say, but probably the only way
scientists will discover worldwide
pollution-free energy
is as a by-product
of war profiteering weaponry.
This is a conspiracy
that threatens all of humanity!
All eyes should be focused
on wireless electricity,
and the complete power
of solar and wind,

not highly explosive,
water-dependent,
natural gas and hydrogen.
And their absurd plan
to excavate the moon
for nuclear hydrogen 3
is another sure sign
of their insanity!
The faster they move,
the further they go.
The more far-reaching
their mobility,
the closer they are
to ending life's ebb and flow.

THE LEANER, MEANER, GLOBAL FREE TRADE ARENA

Here we have a press-excluded
Manhattan event, where over
150 corporate executives
pay up to 1,400 dollars a seat
to learn how to move jobs
out of America more effectively.
Also being raised is the question,
"Is this 'outsourcing' unpatriotic?" [4]
On another self-centered stage,
we had George W. Bush
promising the American people
that if he could remain in power
for a second term,
he would spend millions
of our tax dollars
educating and retraining us
for jobs that "actually exist."
(These were his exact words).
"The key is to train for the work
that actually exists." [5]
At the same time,
this same president
allowed America to lose
over two million jobs.
America is facing
one of the most unstable
economic climates of her existence,
because many of the jobs
that are not securely fastened down
are being moved out of the country,
and many of the jobs
that they find immovable
are being filled
by the illegal immigrants
that they are allowing in.
And to add insult to injury,
those at the top falsely claim

that the American people
can be competitive
in this new global market
if only they educate
or re-educate themselves,
but this is not entirely true,
because no matter how knowledgeable
the American people become,
we cannot compete
with well-educated, low-wage workers.
Even if we were to drown ourselves
in college debt to become,
let's say, a computer programmer,
just take a look at our competition!
In India, the average yearly salary
of a computer programmer is $5,880,
but in the USA, the average annual pay
is $63,331. [6] Should it come as a surprise
to anyone that our high-tech jobs
are outsourced to India?
Aside from the military,
our government should spell out
which "jobs for the 21st century"
we should be educating and training
our children and ourselves for.
Now if they do not choose
to do this voluntarily,
the American people should insist
that our politicians
give us a complete list
of the jobs that "actually exist,"
and then give us a 100% guarantee
that these jobs will not fall victim
to their policies and to their corporate
friends' global economy. If for any reason
they decide not to do this, they should resign
and stop wasting our money and our time!

TRAGEDY AND BETRAYAL

ON THE MOST TREASONOUS SCALE

No one in this country
should be too big to fail!
Our leaders
are a bunch
of bottom feeders,
and their razor-sharp
bankruptcy laws
are just another
one of the ways
that they bleed us.
Now here is a question,
as well as a major life lesson.
Who makes more money?
(A) Microsoft, (B) Exxon Mobile, or
(C) our government on student loans.
The answer is C,
and our politicians
owe us a huge apology.
They cling to a bankroll
on top of the totem pole,
and they're tightening the rope,
and the stool that they have placed
under our feet is called false hope!
They need to loosen the noose
and call a truce
and drastically reduce
our college debt
and the misery index
that they themselves
have built to the hilt!
And if they refuse?
At re-election time,
we should all line up
and make sure they lose!

LITTLE HAS CHANGED

TO DISCREDIT THIS CLAIM FROM FISHER AMES

"It has never happened in the world,
and it never will, that a democracy
has been kept out of the control
of the fiercest and most turbulent
spirits in a society; they will breathe into it
all their own fury, and make it subservient
to the worst designs of the worst men…" [7]
Fisher Ames served in the House of Representatives
for five terms and was a member of the Federalist Party,
as was George Washington and John Adams.
He was also a delegate to the 1788 convention
in Massachusetts that ratified the U.S. Constitution.
His wise words certainly shed light on our present plight!

THE CAUSE

AND EFFECT

Traumatized by what
I've subjected myself to see.
All to unearth the truth
and then reverse its reality.

"The greatness of a nation and its moral progress can be judged by the way its animals are treated."
—Mahatma Gandhi

INVENTORS AT THE CENTER OF THE CRIMINALLY INSANE

This taxpayer-funded,
food and agricultural organization
prefers covert operations
and is free from litigation.
For "All's fair in love and war,"
and for a twin fetish these neo-Nazis
will explore the horror and gore.
Their opinion about dominion
is fanatical at best;
at worst it is an alibi
to be bestially perverse.
Their fixation on sexual mutation
is in fact an act of voyeurism
and masochism and animal mutilation!
Heartbreak hill is synonymous
with this vile, autonomous,
fifty-five mile, prison farm domicile!
As you dine at your customary eating place,
think about me on this abandoned ammunition base.
I am bovine; I am ewe; I am swine.
I am genetically modified
to be premium, choice and prime.
They want me to be large;
they want me to be lean;
they want me to be a freakish baby machine.
I am ruthlessly engineered to fit a mold
where I need not be sheltered
from predators and the cold.
They have replaced my warm wool
with "thin shedding hair"
and have called this mutation
"easy care." [8]

They are so proud
to possess this godlike skill,
but it is demonic in its nature
and it has nothing to do with divine will.
I am treated like an inanimate object
on an assembly line
and forced to endure
multiple operations all at the same time.
They surgically explore
my reproductive system and my brain
and show intense disdain
at the slightest mention of the word "pain."
I am physically and mentally scarred,
while my babies are often abandoned,
crushed and starved.
In this merciless malpractice,
I am lawfully misshaped
and poked, prodded and gang-raped.
I am terrified, abused and in pain,
and I suffer at the hands of Dr. Mengele,
but there is no M.D. in his name.
The design he has in mind,
extracts the greatest profit from us
in the least amount of time.
Oh the death rate; it is high.
We are dropping like flies
and they just stand by and let us die.
This unacceptable, mad scientist experimentation
shows a complete lack of consideration.
They want the full benefits of our domestication;
without the cost, care and aggravation.
Their principles have been blown way off base;
they've deviated from the human race!
Yes, this is where your tax dollars went.
How many of you approve
of how your money is being spent?

WHAT IS WRONG WITH THIS PICTURE

There is ample proof as to why
our trade deficit is sky-high.
Our trade deficit is through the roof
because of brazen tax evasion!
Why did the deregulating
inept reps of our nation
make it the taxpayer's obligation
to pay the import tax,
when they ship all of these
outsourced products back?
Why is it our obligation
and not the outsourcing corporations?
And sixteen billion in federal aid
to General Electric, [9] what's that all about?
Why don't we ask the CEO of GE,
Jeff Immelt, who was then director
of our Federal Reserve,
and while we're at it,
why don't we ask him this?
When it comes to service,
whom do you serve first;
do you serve your nation
or your corporation?
It seems as if he answered this question
without being asked. "When I am talking…
I talk China, China, China, China, China.
You need to be there. You need to change
the way people talk about it and how they get there.
I am a nut on China. Outsourcing from China
is going to grow to $5 billion.
We are building a tech center in China.
Every discussion today has to center on China." … [9]
Can you believe this? He should plead the Fifth!
Jeff Immelt, you said it yourself, you're a nut
and when it comes to moving
our military work to China,
you should be made to keep your mouth shut.
So many problems, so dangerous and so true,

just how many of them
have been hidden from our view?
The American people
have been fed so many lies
that to mislead for self-serving purposes
should come as no surprise.
Propaganda! Propaganda!
It's not just used on communist eyes!
Companies like GE, Verizon
and Apple have thrived,
while the United States of America
has taken a nosedive.
The factory of the future was designed
with only profits in mind!
Why weren't these burgeoning costs
ever entered into the equation?
Evidently, all of their thoughts
were centered on tax evasion!
Now they pay pennies to our dollar.
They live in luxury,
while the majority live in squalor.
They get richer and richer quicker.
In sync, our middle class
gets smaller and smaller.
Our country and our people
are now beset with debt,
and because of a most dishonorable,
unhealthy bond,
our politicians
are impotent to respond.
Apparently, the only thing
they will rise up for
is raising our retirement age;
raising our taxes;
and of course, wagering
and engaging us in war!
Now at last of our government
we must ask, with friends like you,
Who needs enemies?

GLOBAL MANIFEST DESTINY

Inflation rises; selected salaries soar,
while many of us work
one or more jobs and still get poor.
Our companies are closing.
Our healthcare, taxes
and sky-rocketing college debt
are dragging us down,
and lo and behold,
there are hungry, homeless,
uninsured, unemployed
people all around.
Wake Up America!
This raging Global Age
that's been thrust upon us,
with all its viruses
and un-American global job migration,
is not only a threat to our national security
and our once independent nation,
it is also seen by the people
holding the position of supreme power
in America, as an incredible opportunity
to seize foreign frontiers.
But what they don't care to see
is that this time,
it is America being taken here.
America is being taken
piece by piece, patent by patent,
job by job and tax dollar by tax dollar.
America has been left with an eye-popping,
mouth-dropping, record-shattering
trade deficit. And the main reason why?
Because America's once
major exporting companies
are shedding their American employees
like a snake shedding its skin,
and they're migrating to "low pole sites"
and they're importing back in.
The American worker

has become too rich for their blood.
So they are scouring the Earth
for the cheapest labor force
that they can find,
and in the process,
they are leaving America
and our people behind.
Global job migration
is really the exploitation
of poorer nations.
They don't want to help
all these needy impoverished people.
Not the way they've set it up.
There are way too many flaws.
They give no benefits;
they pay poverty wages,
and this one is probably their favorite:
They can operate under lax environmental laws.
Boundless global free trade is a smoke screen,
not a solution,
and it is just what our Mother Earth needs,
more uncontrolled industrialized pollution.
Now America is no longer
a manufacturing nation!
Foreign factory jobs
have all but eliminated
American factory jobs.
Today, the majority
of the mass-produced products
that Americans buy
are cheaply made
in foreign countries.
Made with pride
and built to last
are sadly slipping away
with the past, and just as sadly,
it is now the white collar
worker's turn to get burned.
This transfer of America's wealth
to overpopulated China and India

not only has decimated
our middle class,
it has also made them
our major competitors for fuel,
which is driving up the price
for our goods and gas.
Now if it became necessary
to boycott China,
what would such a sanction be called?
The barefoot, bare-assed, bare-handed,
bored out of our minds boycott?
America is self-sufficient no more!
Greed has booted America's self-sufficiency
out the windows and out the free trade door,
and now in neither material,
nor in our own labor supply
is America at a heightened
readiness for war.
America has too many people
working on our side,
people we have been made to
depend on and trust,
people, some of whom
have a deep-seeded hate for us,
people who in national loyalty
to their own country, in a time of war,
would most certainly try to destroy us.
Since September 11th,
America has come to see,
some of these people
have been working
in our own country.
It is now only a matter of time
before warm becomes cold
and new becomes old,
and America's most valuable
technology has been bought,
stolen, traded and sold.
Where then will America be
and at whose mercy?

IMAGINE WHAT IT WOULD BE LIKE

America is called the land of opportunity
because there are so many ways to succeed,
but this prosperity is being threatened
by the forces of greed.
If only those with power
were forced to feel the full effects
of a displaced worker's despair,
then and only then would the outcries
and the protests be heard loud and clear.
Let's imagine for a moment
that it became fashionable
to replace those in Hollywood
with computer-generated, non-opinionated,
perfect actors and actresses.
What a concept! What a cost-effective idea!
Just think, no more multi-million dollar movie stars.
What would all these pampered people do,
and how much in federal and state income tax
would our U. S. government lose?
But let's not stop there.
What if it was suddenly in style
to hire handsome, foreign-born
news commentators who were completely
Americanized and fully fluent in English,
and they were willing to anchor the news
for ridiculously low wages?
Now let's take it one step further.
What if CEOs and corporate executives,
were systematically replaced by well-educated,
highly motivated, H-1B Visa holders,
and judges, lawyers and lobbyists
were quickly made to realize
that they too were not immune
to this type of job displacement?
How would you feel if all your hard work
and benefits headed south or down the drain?
Would you take comfort in the fact
that it was only "an instant in time" of pain?

"I readily concede there may be an instant in time,
where someone has been pained by free trade." [10]
(These are the quoted words of George W. Bush).
I guess it was only "an instant in time" of pain
for all those people he executed in Texas too.
George W. Bush executed more people
than any other governor in U.S. history
(152 people). [11]   Now let's go too far!
Imagine if we could immediately replace
our politicians with foreigners
who were the most honest,
effective problem solvers in the world,
and their one and only ambition,
their one and only desire
was to do what was best
for our Mother Earth
and all of her inhabitants,
and they were able to do this work
without first brutally building wealth,
without coercing campaign contributions,
and without extra-large bodyguards.
What then? If history is repeated,
with or without bodyguards,
these much loved and needed leaders
would traditionally meet an untimely death.
Oh yeah! There are laws
against holding public office
if you are not a United States citizen.
How convenient for our politicians!
Is this not protectionism?

WE BRING GOOD THINGS TO LIFE

GE, what future have you planned for me?
My family and I are afraid to see.
We work and wait, in a fearful state
because it is our security that is at stake.
You're on the move. You're on the go.
You're on the fast track to many places,
including China, Hungary and Mexico.
We do work for our military,
and it's hard to believe
our government never stopped you;
in fact, they helped you to leave.
Still, you say it's time to pick up the pace
in your global job migration race.
Are you American? Do you care?
It is bad enough you're leaving us behind,
but now you're trying to drag
your vendors down with you there.
Once you and your vendors
have "restructured" and are all long gone,
will the America you left still be as strong?
Now we work for you here,
without a penny to spare
and you always take more
than the contract before.
Lots of us work sleep-deprived
because on a forty-hour income,
we find it hard to survive.
Many of us are too young to retire,
but too old to stray.
Now you're trading us in
for foreign workers;
you pay up to six dollars a day.
You're selling us out
for foreign cheap labor.
You give new meaning
to the saying "Love Thy Neighbor."
Now this is addressed to you, Bill Clinton;
this is why every informed American worker

felt your migrating attack,
when you were off on Martha's Vineyard
playing golf with Neutron Jack.
We do not know to what extent you received,
but if you answered that it was nothing,
that we would never believe.
GE, you say "We Bring Good Things to Life."
Well, this reliance on China
that you influentially helped bring to life
would have been best if it was put to rest.

THE MACHINIST'S PLIGHT

Stress is high. Tolerances are tight.
If you let down your guard,
you can lose a limb or your sight.
Fellow employees have even died
when conditions weren't right.
Around World War II,
we were the highest-paid trade.
There were so many jobs to be had
and a ton of cash to be made.
But somewhere along the line
someone devalued us.
You can now make more money
driving an MBTA bus.
Still, our armed forces depend
on the aircraft engines that we make.
Outsourcing should be illegal
when our soldier's lives are at stake.
How irresponsible, unpatriotic and disloyal
that our military work
is being cheaply manufactured
on foreign soil.
America's military work
should have always been a different story.
Manufacturing it here should be mandatory!
Now the rest of us work out on the floor,
where it's hot as hell.
How much time do we have left?
Only time will tell.
In their suits and their ties,
they have it made in the shade.
Their boundless global free trade passed.
Now it's us and American Made that they trade.
Today when our fellow American workers
lose their jobs, due to global, mobile free trade,
they are rhetorically classified as displaced.
Displaced, replaced, pushed aside,
taken on a reckless "Manifest Destiny" ride.
No matter what they call it,

no matter what they say,
the American people need to know
that our jobs are being traded away
to foreign workers who are so poor,
they will do our work for no benefits
and next-to-nothing pay.
Now to the workers who replace us,
what can I say?
I am not angry with you in any way.
I am sad, and I feel bad
that they are making all of us live this way.
War rages in technological stages
because our world is dependent
on military industrial wages.
What a costly expense
to make dollars instead of sense!

THE DECEITFUL ARTIST OF ALLOCUTION

Bill Clinton, I believed you.
I thought you cared.
I thought you understood.
I thought America
had finally found a leader
who was looking out
for our best interests.
Because you wore your heart
upon your sleeve,
for all to witness, for all to see,
and what a painful reality to find,
the welfare of America's workers
couldn't have been
any further from your mind.
At least with George H. W. Bush,
we knew where we stood;
we knew where his loyalty resided.
He had a strong loyalty
like Robin Hood, only in reverse,
and one of the reasons he wasn't re-elected is
we knew he would have left us
with the NAFTA free trade curse.
But you, Bill Clinton,
you took the protective stance,
that if you were elected,
the American workforce
would have a fighting chance.
But then you voted in favor
of what you were supposed to be opposing.
You were nothing more
than a wolf in sheep's clothing.
Now for you and all you've put us through,
should America shout hooray?
Did your NAFTA Free Trade save the day?
Just look up! Look down!
There's backlash all around!
What a price we have paid

for not-so-free trade. What a cost!
Countless American jobs lost!
You said we should be happy with the jobs
that NAFTA Free Trade has made,
but they can never compare to the vital jobs
you've taken away from us here.
Now our much-needed jobs,
lost forever, are staring us in the face
and you helped do this to us,
and it is truly a disgrace.
It will be no mystery when these events
and your Presidency appear
on one of the most shameful pages
in America's history.
Speaking of history, it's been said
that you have compared yourself
to Theodore Roosevelt, and this is true,
but only of opposite acts.
He built this country up!
You let this country down!
And if you were present and in power,
during the Progressive Era,
and you tried to throw our people
into the global age, especially with China,
you would have been dragged
into the street and stoned,
and I don't mean the kind of stoned
where you smoke but don't inhale.
Now please forgive me,
if being dragged into the street and stoned
was out of date and rightfully out of reach,
but for your Benedict Arnold behavior
of **empowering and arming** Asia,
you would have at least been impeached.
If I only knew all the damage you would do,
I never would have voted for you.
After all I now know,
I am left wondering if America
would have been better off with Ross Perot.
Now to the Vice President

who failed to succeed,
you can only distance yourself
from the president's sexual deeds.
Bill Clinton and Al Gore,
what did you set America up for?
Boom, Slump, War!

Jack Welch, also known as Neutron Jack,
Chairman and CEO of General Electric,
retired from GE in 2001 and presently
teaches business students his philosophy,
which has been labelled "The Welch Way."

THE WELCH WAY

Imagine being as ruthless
as Jack Welch and being proud of it.
Having the power to hire and fire
and getting endowed from it.
He moved his workers
like they were on an assembly line
in the combat zone,
where "what's yours is mine
and what's mine is my own."
And this is the role model
our business world is supposed to follow?
Too bad Jack Welch didn't find it worthwhile
to reward his rank and file,
and not just himself and his lavish lifestyle.
But that's a fantasy; that's a joke.
Jack Welch doesn't give a damn
about the working folk.
Spreading the wealth and wanting to share
is only a concern if you really care,
but you don't! That is why you took
the largest retirement severance payment in history.
"$417 million" dollars, [12] not to mention
a nine-million-dollar annual pension, [13]
an $80,000-a-month Manhattan Central Park apartment,
and many other luxuries: including wining, dining,
flowers, limos and phones. Plus furniture, computers
and Internet and maid service, at your multiple homes.
You're just living it up, with lifetime use of a company jet,
free membership in the most exclusive country clubs, and
courtside and box seats to topnotch sporting events. [14]
Then in a nonstop drop from the top,
you swear that you are being more than fair

when you force your elderly GE retiree
with thirty-four and half years' service
to live on a paltry pension of $530.00 a month, [15]
with no cost-of-living provision in place.
Let's not forget to mention
that this measly monthly pension
is the gross amount before deductions
for medical benefits and taxes.
We do the back-breaking work
and you get the money and all the perks.
What a greedy, egotistical jerk!
A team is like a well-oiled machine,
where all the parts work as one
to get the job done.
But you don't see it that way.
You only see the top one and the top two.
You don't care to see the hell
that you are putting the rest of us through.
Jack Welch, your excessive desire
to be number one has also robbed us
of precious moments with our daughters and sons.
These moments are irretrievable,
and your ruthless, stop-at-nothing attitude
and these key words that you went ahead
and said to Lou Dobbs is unbelievable.
"Ideally you'd have every plant
you own on a barge"…
That way you can barge
in and out of countries
and use their workers
as your poverty wage slaves.
The ruthless robber baron
of long ago is now called a CEO!
It is so well-known, and over and over again
it has been shown that this sort of man
will shamelessly exploit
our Mother Earth's natural resources.
Yes, like a savage he will ravage her
for his own gain.
Now unfortunately this is old

and nothing new
and just as unfortunately,
American and foreign workers
are merely natural resources too.
Jack Welch, you want for nothing.
You have it all.
Your boundless global free trade passed.
Now America is taking the fall.
But what do you care?
You're filthy rich.
You're set for life.
You can retire and live
happily ever NAFTA.
I hope when you meet your maker
and witness your full life review,
you experience the hardship
that you have put your workers
and their families through.

TOO MANY UNLUCKY NUMBERS

MERGERS AND ACQUISITIONS

With a merger here and a merger there,
you throw people's lives up in the air.
Then you coldly and calculatingly
kick back and watch
as your loyal employee's livelihood,
identity, and safety net all at once disappears.
You're like a powerful catalyst in a pot.
You aggressively stir things up.
Then you stand alone and call all the shots.
Once the two of you are legally one,
you systematically cut your workforce way back.
Then you force your remaining employees
to pick up the slack.
First you pay our politicians for your success.
Then ultimately, you make everyone else
pay more for less.
Merging and marching,
they're one and the same.
You're marching toward a monopoly
in this money making-game.
But you see no victims;
greed has made you deaf,
dumb and blind.
You only see us as numbers
that you've left behind.
And unfortunately for us,
there is only one number
that is all too important to you.
How shameful the things you have done,
all to attain this insane number one.
Your philosophy will always be:
We're not making enough money;
we can't compete. You won't be happy
until the whole world is at your feet!

A DISEMBODIED-VOICE DREAM

It's been said you were called ungrateful in bed.
Our great grandparents came to you in a dream.
Some were quite angry, some were quite mean.
They spoke for hours and hours it seemed.
Their spirits were uneasy; they no longer could rest,
because for their country,
you were not doing what was best.
The first voice you heard was stern and strong,
and when he spoke, you immediately knew
you had done something wrong.
"You have caused us much pain
and you have brought us nothing but shame,
and all on account of you,
a declaration of dependence
is now a more fitting claim.
We were once the inventors and the producers
of the products we would use and sell,
but the grandest thing of all,
we were once self-sufficient as well,
but then without ever giving
the American people a say,
someone greedy for bribes,
gave you the almighty power
to live for today
and sell America's future away.
You have weakened America
and have left us in despair.
We have been watching you, son,
take our jobs far from here.
These are the jobs
that put you through school.
These are the jobs
that helped you to rule.
But to you it's a game; it's a sport.
How many of our jobs
will you be allowed to export?
Your pledge of allegiance
to our country is clearly none.

We deeply regret not instilling
this most important quality in you, son.
You are a 'lover of yourself
and not given to reason,'
and each time you push and pass
boundless global free trade,
you are committing borderline treason.
Now we are not saying importing is wrong,
but we all know manufacturing here
made America strong
and it is to our offspring
that these jobs do belong.
Just take a look at life
from our point of view.
We worked harder
so you wouldn't have to.
Then what do you go and do
with your success?
You eliminate our jobs
and call it progress.
We are calling upon you now
to give back what you have taken
and to favor
the United States of America
which you have forsaken."
Then as you awoke
and their voices
were fading away,
it's been said,
these were the last words
you heard them say.
"We fear the Trojan Horse
of Troy, once done,
may soon be visiting you, my son.
Start on a clean slate
and pray it is not too late."

THE TERRAIN HAS CHANGED

This overpowering,
job-devouring,
third world nation,
exploitation,
with its overarching TPP,
along with the conflict
in the South China Sea,
just might march us
into World War III.
Again and again,
the curtain was closed,
but we were too misguided
and divided
to stop mobile
global free trade
from being imposed.
Now behold
this ephemeral gold
that they hold;
it has become
a bloody ivory tower
with China
as an adversarial
super power.
Is this a blame game
or Russian roulette?
One thing is for sure,
this is a Mad Max threat!

OUTRAGEOUS ACCOLADES
OF THE POACHER'S TRADE

Boundless global free trade
created both crushing poverty
and a vast, elite consumer class,
which tragically features
the mass slaughter
of our Earth's most endangered species.
Tiger-bone wine; an elephant's tusk,
a rhino's horn, a seal's dick,
man, if that's what you need to breathe,
you're bloody sick!

THE HIDDEN FEE

OF AN I-DOLLAR-TREE ECONOMY
OR IS IT PRONOUNCED IDOLATRY

For thrills and dollar bills and factory mills
they have danced like puppets on Capitol Hill.
First came the conspiring, firing bleat
from the greedy puppeteers on Wall Street.
Things were exchanged and arranged,
and then the trade name was picked
and our independence channel got clicked.
Along with the pink slips and the axe,
they raised prices and every imaginable tax
and even distorted the reporting of the facts.
But they still have some jobs to kill.
Yes, they have some robbed jobs to fill.
You know that Ross Perot
and that giant sucking sound?
Now we're losing common ground
and we're far from safe and sound.
We're still reeling from the effects
and here comes the next hex.
Even though trust is a must,
bonds have been broken.
So it's not so surprising
that temperatures are rising.
Now their jaws are wide open
and some hearts are closed,
and another World War
just might take its toll.
Too bad they didn't look past the fast cash
to see that this is not worth peace on Earth.
The opposite behavior of "Love Thy Neighbor"
has been going on for so long and it is wrong!
We want peace, not war!
We want to be middle class, not poor.
We need a safe occupation,
one that is free from toxins and intimidation,
one that is not founded on exploitation,

one that includes respect and appreciation.
All of us need to be needed,
but above all, we all need love.
Surely, if we were a blood relation,
we would not be subjected to this dehumanization.
This abuse and neglect and lack of respect
have had a disastrous effect.
Including violence and hate
and an escalating, heart-breaking suicide rate.
Now if we were to grade our leaders
on a compassionate scale;
most of them would not pass, they would fail.
Our Earth and everything on it
should be cared for and loved.
Then there would be no need
to anesthetize ourselves with drugs.
Life is for living,
and hearts and hands are for giving.
Once our leaders learn this lesson,
life won't be a curse. It will be a blessing.

A FALLING STAR

What happens to us
is not who we are,
just as the act of falling
is not the star.

THE ME GENERATION

Many of the people holding the position
of supreme power in America
epitomize the "Me Generation."
And it's all about me, and power and penetration.
And it's all about me, and money and manipulation.
It's all glitz and glamour, get my needs met;
betray the American people
and put them deeper and deeper in debt.
Theodore Roosevelt once said,
"Politicians who betray the American trust
must be exposed and corrupt businessmen
must be prosecuted."
Now come one! Come all! Let the show begin!
In some cases, America's judicial system
has become a three-ring circus,
where fair and impartial
are not always allowed to win.
We are all at the mercy of a few
who have never whole-heartedly felt
that all men and women are created equal.
They think of themselves
as coming from a much higher descent,
and it is their true belief
that it is their high-powered right
that everyone born beneath them
should cater to and serve them
on their "pursuit for life, liberty and happiness."
They are many in our American government;
they are many in multinational corporate America.
And they not only have
the right connections,
they are totally connected!
And as their one hand
has always washed the other,
it has always been the rest of us
that they have taken to the cleaners.

MERCURY IN RETROGRADE

Integrity is missing from this equation
and that explains the degradation.
What's the angle? What's the function?
Planned Obsolescence equals endless consumption!
What a waste having to replace
something that we couldn't afford in the first place.
Now plastic is the new metal and that's no mistake,
because even the necessities of life
are designed to crack and brake.
They want to make money
more than they want to save lives.
So they will lie and cheat
and they will drag their feet,
and they will stall on issuing a recall
until their backs are up against the wall,
and when somebody dies it's not a crime;
they just settle out of court or pay a fine,
but one thing they'll never do is do any time,
and the punishment doesn't fit the crime.
How can economic conditions ever be ideal
when it's the richest of the rich
that beg, borrow and steal?
They are fleecing every person's pocket
and they are killing people and profiting off of it.
Now weapons have been dispersed
to the ends of the earth
and can be dated back
to the manufacturer of the attack.
Then on cue, what do we do?
We seek out the highest high
to counter the great weight
of the lowest of lows,
knowing that the choices
that our leaders have chosen
could bring life
as we know it to a close.
Now we're racking up a tab in rehab
and what else is new;

they're profiting off of that too.
We are sick of suffering
the wear and tear
and the emotional drain
of being knee-deep in a world
that is filled with fear and pain,
and we are sick and tired
of being led by leaders
who are liars and cheaters.
Now let the liars be quiet
and the truth be told;
you are a cancer to your country
if you can be bought or sold!

THE DEN OF AMERICA'S POLITICAL MIDDLEMEN

THIS CAN PERTAIN TO WOMEN, AS WELL

Is America going to hell
in a campaign contribution handbag?
It's been said the Clintonites
did their soliciting over breakfast,
lunch and coffee,
and golfing and jogging
was their way to foreplay.
And if the price was right,
you could even bed
at the White House overnight.
Every fiber of our American being
rapidly eroded
at the shameful, hungry hand
of the Clinton/Gore Administration
and unscrupulous Democrats
and Republicans alike.
Many of them
are like powerful pimps
and powerless prostitutes
who will do anything,
no matter how dirty
or under-handed,
all for the love of power,
prestige and legalized PAC money.
And the more you show,
the lower they'll go.
But "as sure as death and taxes,"
they will always say,
"That's not me! That's not me!"
Then off they go
where they hope no one will see.
"It wasn't me! It wasn't me!"
Well if not you, then who?
Your evil twin Duplicity!
In the Holy Bible, it is said,

"Do not pervert justice
or show partiality."
"Do not accept a bribe,
for a bribe blinds the eyes of the wise
and twists the words of the righteous."
It is also said, "A bribe is a charm
to the one who gives it;
wherever he turns, he succeeds."
In other words,
if you feed powerful greed
you will succeed.
Apparently, this type of behavior
is nothing new
and it was not just put into play.
It has always been that way.
To the end and from the start,
the power-hungry
have been consumed
by their gluttonous heart.
Ronald Reagan proved my point perfectly
when he said, "Politics is supposed to be
the second oldest profession.
I have come to realize
it bears a very close
resemblance to the first." (16)
(The first being prostitution.)
Well on this one,
Ronald Reagan was right.
He knew the score
and it's pleasing to the rich,
but it's multiplying the poor.

THE PRESENT STATE

Health, wealth, age, aspects
emotions, tendencies and traits,
along with past experiences,
accumulate to make up the present state.

READ MY LIPS I NEVER LIE

I'M AS SWEET AS ALL - AMERICAN APPLE PIE

2000 was an election year like no other year.
We were at the dawn of the millennium,
and the outcome of this presidential election
was more than many could bear.
Now the exact effect this rejected elect
would have on our future was still unclear.
But one thing was for sure, both Bush and Gore
were symptomatic of America's ailments;
they weren't the remedy or the cure.
America is in a state of upheaval
and what do we have here?
An unacceptable, pandering, two-party power
that doesn't know how to play fair!
With billions of dollars **wasted**,
countless deals are made.
By the divided, powerless people,
the price will be paid and paid.
This road that career politicians travel,
big business has paved in gold bricks,
and what most politicians have up their sleeves
is campaign-selling tricks.
Now is it my imagination, or am I so aware,
some of these politicians
are falling all over themselves,
just to convince us they really care,
and in the same movement,
they're successfully blocking the critical issues
and the third party candidates,
for they fear they'll lose
if they let democracy shine through here?
And all because of party loyalty,
many voters have chosen not to see
that the majority of Democrats
and Republicans are 0 for 3
when it comes to long term
reliability and integrity.

Don't you know? Once they win,
for you, they no longer care.
Once they're in,
their promises and predictions,
along with their loyalty
and compassion for you,
disappear into thin air.
There are not many things in life
you can count on,
but this one is tried and true,
your politicians will only show
devotion when they need you.
Then in the course of time,
when their mighty, thoughtless decisions
bring you down to your knees,
and you once looked up to them,
but now you no longer like what you see;
don't look for changes.
It'll take another insincere election year
before it's you they aim to please.
And alas, what should we all now see?
An incredibly corrupt catastrophe!
Al Gore lost to the energy industry!
But most importantly,
what each and every one of us should now see,
is that we are nothing more than bystanders
of a mass society, being sold the fantasy
that we are living in the land of democracy.
Plutocracy, as well as **Pandering**
and **Gerrymandering,**
have seized too strong
a foothold on our Democracy.
Now our once independent nation,
is again habitually caught
in a vicious cycle of reciprocation.
And for what? Preferential Treatment!
That is what this ruling minority requires.
And for this privilege they have
greedily done their part,
and they are now leading America

down the road to ruin
and tying our newly elected
officials' hands from the start.
Yes, what we have here,
is too many special interest groups
filling too many election-hungry hands,
expecting these politicians at a later date
to cave into their demands.
Now let's note, some will
and some won't,
but there's no denying
the rich get the most favored votes
and the lower classes don't.
Now let only their real record
speak and defend itself
and if they don't have a record,
they shouldn't be running.

THE PROBLEM
WITH IMPERFECT POWER

THEY SHOW NO MERCY

The majority of the holders
of the vast wealth in this world
has given no future to philanthropy.
They have selfishly and self-servingly
kept it in its infancy.
Yet, they have willingly and wantonly
let poverty and despair
grow well past full maturity.
If only **Love** were perceived
as the most valuable treasure of all,
poverty would become a thing of the past,
because then those who have finished first in life
would have the **compassion** to move forward those
who have been pushed to the back.

QUESTIONING COMPETITION WITHIN THE COLONY

ANOTHER BEE ANALOGY

What if a bee inflicted wounds
on himself and the others to be the best?
Wouldn't that separate him from the rest?
And wouldn't this unwanted exclusion
cause him pain and confusion?
Now what if this condition
were highly contagious,
and this behavior became normal
instead of outrageous?
Wouldn't pride multiply and divide
making it increasing difficult
to work equally side by side?
If equal opportunity
were to be lost in their community,
wouldn't the gap between superiority
and inferiority weaken their unity?
Now if this is actually taking place
within the human race,
how long will it be
before the good of the whole
spirals completely out of control?

A UNIQUE CULTURAL CRITIQUE

In this age, everyone is taught
youth is in and aging must be fought.
Our culture is fixated
on the body and face,
and anything short of perfection
is considered a fall from grace.
There was a time
when pleasantly plump
and well-fed meant well-bred,
but this is no longer the case.
We have been reduced
to a life of skin and bones.
Our food supply is laced
with pesticides, chemicals and hormones.
And we are idolized or demoralized
depending on our body size.
The stage is set. The table is cleared.
Dazed and confused, we're ushered
into the most intoxicating atmosphere.
Food, liquor, violence and sex
flash across the screen.
Divided and **Conquered**,
our very being grumbles,
hungry and mean.
Our society is now sickened,
saddened and suicidal
and everything in between.
When will we stop this madness?
Who will intervene?

A FALSE IMAGE

Selling an image
of superimposed perfection
casts a reflection
of real self-rejection.
Over and over,
and over again,
the mass media
distorts the body images
of women, children and men.
What do you say?
What do you do?
How do you feel?
When it's your needed
self-esteem that they steal?
They hook and reel
with sex appeal.
Half of which isn't even real!
What a money-making deal!
It's predacious
as well as salacious.
They are the hunter
and we're their target.
They are the harlot
and we're their market.
They bait the hook
with enhanced looks
and then they lure.
If I had fewer morals,
I'd rhyme with more.

THE ANIMA AND THE ANIMUS

Each of us has an opposite side that we hide,
that we're afraid to let ourselves and others see
because in our society,
it is seen as either weak or ugly.
Yet, we are magnetically drawn
to its purposeful power and beauty.
In females, it can be
the masculine trait of assertiveness.
In males, it can be
the feminine side of sensitivity.
This must be why we often hear the reply
Don't be a bitch, or Big boys don't cry.

GUARANTEED AUTHENTIC

IN THE BEGINNING

We are born into this world
naked, innocent and absent of armor,
but as we grow,
we progressively develop
defensive coverings and masks
to protect and conceal
the open wounds and scars
that we've received
when we've revealed to others
who we really are.

ARE WE AUTHENTIC OR NOT

A tree is a tree.
A mountain is a mountain.
A river is a river.
A wild animal is a wild animal.
And the list goes on and on.
Nothing false is added.
Nothing true withdrawn.
Only mankind has sought
to make himself and others
something they are not.
And stress, insecurity
and suffering are the result!

THE BLEEDING HEART

When we mistake what we want for what we need,
we create insufficiency, fear and parasitic greed.
As a result, we give up what we love
for what we think we need, and in the process,
instead of being nurtured and nourished, we bleed.
Looking back, what was it that we loved to do,
that fell by the wayside, as our insecurities grew?
What was our passion? What did we hold dear?
What did we abandon out of ignorance and fear?
If there were only one answer, it would be **Nature!**

A LOSS OF SPIRIT

A BLEEDING HEART LEADS TO A LOSS OF SPIRIT

A loss of Spirit lessens the lines
of communication with our Soul,
and from this abyss we have an energy crisis.
A severed circuitry between our Spirit and Soul
will leave us overly hungry and out of control.
Our Spirit and Soul are our life force; our energy source.
Together, they are ours to enrich, uplift and console,
but when we choose not to, it tragically takes its toll.

THE DISCOVERY OF FULL RECOVERY

OR GLOOM AND DOOM

Just as we long to keep our body,
thoughts and emotions pure
and struggle to find
our addicted drug-craving cure,
the same type of mind game
is being played out
with our planet's earth, water and air.
And the fact that we have had
such a negative impact on our environment
is causing us the most overwhelming,
heart-wrenching despair.
Amid the oil slicks and time bomb ticks
and our one last fix, the cause and effect
deeply reflect our spiritual disconnect.
We poison ourselves; we poison our planet;
we're venomous! But unlike poisonous snakes
and other such creatures, we can change,
but we must want to and believe wholeheartedly
that we can, or this may be, along with weaponry,
the downfall of man. Now for those of you
who are turning to heroin as a new vice,
think twice. Heroin won't make you happy.
It won't make you a hero. It will make you dead.
It will make you a zero. It'll hook ya,
cook ya and sink ya. Six feet under
and it's no wonder; it's a lethal injection,
run for protection. It's been said Al Qaeda
flooded our streets with smack
in a pandemic narcotic terrorist attack.
It has also been said,
Satan knows his days
are numbered now
and he's trying to hook
as many as he can, and how.
With the prick of this pin,
once that tainted needle goes in,

your painful dance of death begins.
Now when someone tries to tempt you
and you don't know what to do,
turn towards your Lord
to strike the right chord.
And always remember,
an addiction is a catch 22.
You're damned if you don't,
you're damned if you do.
And the damned that I am referring to,
is the living hell the addiction itself
will put you and your family through.

SUFFERING STANDING STILL

This unbearable dissatisfaction
has a productive purpose;
it's pushing us into action.
How long will we suffer standing still?
What will it take to overcome
this weakness of the will?
There is no drug. There is no potion.
The only remedy is forward motion.

A BEE ANALOGY

Their specialization
is the act of pollination.
Ours is the gathering
and dissemination of information,
but in our struggle to counteract
what we **believe** we lack,
we frequently experience
suffering setbacks.
We waste so much energy
and create such unwanted friction
when we continually insist
on orbiting around our addictions.
We need to refocus
and stop playing this unfruitful game
of chasing after sex, drugs, money,
material, food and fame,
along with wanting the perfect body
and face to remain an everlasting claim.
In other words, without fail,
we need to stop chasing our own tail.
What if bees only circled the honey in their hive?
Without pollination, would our planet survive?
Just as making honey is less important
to the survival of our planet than pollination,
our making money is less important
to the health of our planet
than all of us using open communication
to halt the generation of global devastation.
Right now, what our species needs more than ever
is to become emotionally intelligent, not clever.
You cannot throw an ecosystem out of whack
and not expect it to swing wildly back,
but the perpetrators debate and deny
and say that man-made climate change
is a hoax or lie. The proof is in the air;
the poison is in the water and ground
and humanity cannot expect to correct
the ill effect without making a sound.

So speak up! But remember,
words can be weapons. So choose them wisely.
Choose words that move and stir up the mind
and expose the truth and give sight to the blind.
And like pencils, words should be sharpened to a point!

A VESTED INTEREST

If you bow down and worship me,
I will give you power, prestige and money.
If you bow down and worship me,
I will give you an ancient stored form of energy.
Now when you hear of wars, and rumors of wars,
look for the concealed, high yield,
vested interest of the energy field.
And where is another one of their scary 'hot spots'?
It is in the area of Syria! This is a gas pipeline plan,
where opposing forces are waging war
over limited resources. This is the Mark of Cain,
where opposing forces are imposing eminent domain!
Yes, this is more a war over energy,
and less about what we're allowed to see on TV.
Nevertheless, we do not see lines
being drawn in the sand, or the shockwaves
that have sent loved ones fleeing from the land,
and we didn't see what the soldier saw.
So we've never seen the 'shock and awe.'
One thing is clear to see, fighting over energy,
that includes the barbaric act of slavery,
has made us more enemies than friends.
And scarier and scarier, and scarier still,
brutality has been heightened to six-six-six
since Al-Qaeda and ISIS entered the mix.
This behavior is barbaric
and we need to ban it from our planet!
Sadly, sanctuaries of asylum
can no longer clearly see
a traumatized, innocent refugee.
Instead, they see a dorsal fin.
So they're afraid to let them in.
This is crazy! We need to turn this ship
around before we all drown!
This is not how life is meant to end!
Countless soldiers and civilians
have been injured and have died,
because this dangerous, ancient energy supply.

And those who stand to gain,
stand furthest from the pain.
People are afraid of dinosaurs,
just as people are afraid of wars.
Still, being petrified is justified,
because we're being consumed by them now.
Yes, through their fossil fuel,
they are saying, "let's chow!"
This is the most archaic form of modernism!
And it flies in the face of patriotism!
Everyone needs energy to be free,
for without it, we will cease to be.
Besides, we need it, to get from point A to point B.
We also need it to be an educated society.
Plus fossil fuels are a despotic, catastrophic narcotic,
and they're unsustainable! So it's a no brainer;
this should be on the mind and tongue
of every campaigner and entertainer.
Yes, through mic and on the page,
let Wisdom reign, like a revivifying rain
that soothes this needless suffering and pain.
Why are our leaders so resistant to change?
They need to start thinking more long-range.
The USA put the first man on the Moon.
Not to profit off it. Not to run away.
Now we have the Technology, and the Wisdom
to create a Symbiotic Energy System.
NASA can do it and so can GE,
thanks to Tesla, Faraday, and the USA's
space travel technology. Then we can end
this dead end economics and petro aggression,
and petro politics. What are our leaders waiting for?
The last day, the final hour, when their deeds on Earth
are sifted like flour! Or maybe another Halliburton
style of war that our world can still ill afford!
Our leaders, they're either going to save us,
or take us to the grave.
The question is, are they brave enough
to make our innovative nation
a great source of illumination?

"Today, species are going extinct at the fastest rate since the mass extinction of the dinosaurs." [17]

THE REIGN OF CAIN

The Story of Creation
and all its implications
was somehow lost
in the translation.
Likewise, subdued
and being annihilated
are not related.
Man has misconstrued
why nature was created.
The faithful must side
with being Able,
which is attainable.
On the other hand,
if we are not capable,
man's extinction is inescapable.

THE WAR AGAINST THE WORLD

There is a Creation Story
that the Earth was made for man
and she belongs to man alone.
This misread belief
entitles him to kill his competition
and to take everything for himself.
No planet, no animal, no forest,
no body of water; no other form of life
has the right to live or has any value,
unless it is in the service of man.
But even this is not enough.
Here we have a dilemma,
another war of sorts,
for man does not like to share,
not even with mankind,
so he created division.
The question now stands before us,
which type of man
has inherited the right
to rule and conquer the Earth,
and which one has not?
What race, what religion,
what gender, what class,
what region of the world
will win out in the end?
The problem here
is there are no winners, only losers.
This war that modern man
has waged against the world,
and against women and children
and against mankind
must be resolved
if we are to evolve.
There are laws of nature,
to which even these
alpha males must comply,
and if they do not,
we will all eventually die.

THE INDIGENOUS,
THE ENDANGERED,
THE LINK TO THE EXTINCT

Oh, to be left to live off the land.
Oh, to be free from the threat of man.
Oh, to be a priceless part of our Earth.
Oh, to equal or outweigh
the value of economic worth.
We must reverse this curse
of economic worth here on Earth!

ONCE THE BLOOD IS WASHED AWAY

ONLY THE SOFT FUR REMAINS

Bleeding, screaming, writhing in pain,
many of us are skinned alive for ill-gotten gain.
Humanity is against this commercial hunt.
Why won't you stop?
Have you no compassion, not even a drop?
I saw something I shouldn't have seen.
I saw the savagery of a human being.
Oh Canada, Oh Canada, you are not my friend,
for you subsidize and refuse
to bring this seal hunt to an end.
Look into my eyes. What do you see?
I want to live! I'm just a baby!
Reverse this price you've placed upon my head
and save us all from this unnecessary bloodshed.
Soon, a cruel spiked club
will be used to crush my skull,
and you callously call this heinous act a cull.
My flesh will be torn from my body
not for food, but for show.
This should haunt the wearer of the garment
wherever they go. Oh, how greed
has swept love and gentleness away.
Now you no longer see life, you only see prey.
What a cruel world! What a hostile place!
What did we do to incur the wrath of the human race?
Now my eyes are filled with unspeakable fear and dread
as I helplessly wait my turn to stain the snow red.
I call out to the others, but my cries are in vain,
because they too are crying and dying in pain.
Oh the pain! Oh the sorrow!
The last today! The last tomorrow!
Oh Canada, Oh Canada, please be my friend.
You have the power to bring this tragedy to an end.

LIFE REDUCED TO A DOLLAR

Love is absent, blood is everywhere.
Raw consumerism and terror fill the air.
In this cold and violent atmosphere
their sweet disposition cannot appear.
Nor would we want it to,
for that would be too painful to see.
How much easier,
to slaughter a filthy beast of burden
than our beloved companion Lassie?

FOOD FOR THOUGHT

Our artery-hardening,
elite meat diet
may be reduced,
but it is highly unlikely
to be brought to a close.
However, the industrial
factory farm industries'
lack of respect
and barbaric treatment
of these poor animals
must be confronted
and vehemently opposed.
And to those who have ignored
Temple Grandin, you are the first
ones that should be branded.

THE CONVEYOR BELT / THE SHOOT

THE MECHANIZATION OF TURNING LIVESTOCK INTO LOOT

The factory farm industry has cornered the market
and has made itself look picturesque.
They spend more money on PR
and lobbying than cleaning up their bloody mess.
Yes, hidden from view is the pain and suffering
that these poor animals have to go through,
and satisfying a greedy bestial body
cannot be used as an excuse
for dishing out such abuse.
Imagine if human beings found themselves
at the bottom end of the food chain
because a cunning, carnivorous creature
had a superior brain with much to gain?
Being homemade would certainly not have
the same savory appeal
if it was our own flesh and blood
that was being served as the meal.
Now let us set the scene
where we are crammed in like a sardine
and ripped from limb to limb
at this dangerous creature's whim.
Think about our shortened lives
lived in a sickening state,
where we're forced to grow
and gestate at an excessive rate.
Think about the net, the hook,
the club, the crowded crate.
Picture yourself
at the blood-soaked slaughtering gate.
Now envision that you are being pushed
to the breaking point
as your beak is cut to the quick,
and your nails are severed at the joint.
With no pain relief in sight,
would you think that this routine was right?

This is the real visceral material
from which horror movies are made!
How much less entertaining,
if it was your blood that they were draining?
How would we feel, if we were reduced
to a calorie count, a unit or measure,
where our only purpose in life
was to bring another species pleasure?
Would we be so complacent and subdued,
if our family were the main source of food?
Shouldn't this tragic cause give us pause,
to enact much stricter and more humane laws?

NOBODY IS 100% POSITIVE

THE KEY TO NEGATIVITY

How weary to be both you and me,
falling short of who we want to be,
running from what we do not want to see.
How can we escape from our reality of duality?
Living up to an ideal image that society creates
is like trying to find balance in altered states.
First, we must question our perception
of good or bad. Then from there,
we must find the correct time
to subtract or add. Positive or negative,
whichever direction an action is deemed, the key
to our becoming proactive is to avoid all extremes!

JOINED OPPOSITION

Positive and negative are opposites.
Tense energy forms when they interact.
The world would be stuck
in a non-state of neutral
if there were not opposites to attract.
Opposites are not only necessary for procreation;
the tension they produce
is a balancing system of self-regulation.
For instance, through each conflict we enter
we are given the opportunity
to move back toward our center.
Opposites are not separate;
they are perfectly joined,
like reversed sides of the same coin.
What must we encounter
to come to the conclusion
that duality is an illusion?

FAITH IN THE FACE OF FEAR

IS THE ANSWER TO EVERY PRAYER
FOR FEAR FREEZES BUT FAITH FREES

Head lowered in defeat.
Habits activated by fear
are bitter, not sweet.
The buzz, the stupor,
tried to soar high.
Clipped wings cannot fly.
Face fear, now try.
Infinity is before you.
Failure is a lie.
Greater heights are shown
to those who push past
fear of the unknown.
But do not try
to reach too high.
Instead reach
just over your head.

GOD IS LOVE

AND MAN MUST EVOLVE
TO FIT LOVE'S IMAGE

God may have made man
in his own image,
but we still have a long uphill climb,
for the levels of love in our Creator
are unquestionably greater.
Now if each and every one of us
were to write a list,
as to what we want and need,
and how we feel,
would the list look
something like this?
We feel lonely and sad.
We feel betrayed and mad.
We feel love and hate.
We feel we have the right
to judge and rate.
We feel we know the difference
between right and wrong.
We have an overwhelming need
to be accepted and to belong.
And because of deep deprivation,
we need much inspiration,
motivation and vindication.
And because many incite
and say it is alright
to do wrong to fit in,
we have an urgent need
to keep our children safe,
and to be careful
when we discipline.
We need to get involved.
We need to let go.
We need to seek out knowledge
and then we grow.

When we feel superior though,
we are brought low.
When we feel compassion,
we show good will.
When we feel fear,
we lash out and we kill.
We need our privacy.
We want to be alone.
We need to be noticed.
We want to be known.
We feel jealous
and we expect,
assume, or believe,
that we will be happy
and then we grieve.
We mourn so deeply;
there is almost no end
to our sorrow.
Yet, we cling to the hope
of a brighter tomorrow.
Our Earth is able to give us all
that we basically need,
but she is constantly hindered
by economic selfishness,
aggression and greed.
Only when we unite the divided
by making the two equal-sided,
will we create a generous atmosphere
for all to share, but how do we unite
the divided by making the two equal-sided?
We must strengthen our faith
to counter the weight of our fear.
We must cultivate compassion
and show how much we care.
We must raise our vibration
through meditation and prayer,
and we must love ourselves
and one another as one would
a close sister or brother!
Until then, with this "us versus them" mentality

we will be plagued by the commonality
of the most shocking, inhumane brutality.
Everything alive has to evolve to survive,
including us; we are not exempt!
Now, if we are to evolve,
we must make our list
of loving traits so much longer
and our feelings of genuine love
and compassion so much stronger.
It is no accident that LOVE
is found in both the first and last
four letters of the word EVOLVE!

I AM A LEXIGRAM

There are riddles,
there are runes,
there are mysteries to solve.
Love is the hidden meaning
in the word Evolve.
There are riddles,
there are rules,
there are mysteries to solve.
Love is the hidden meaning
in the word Evolve.

LOVE DOES NOT HATE OR DISCRIMINATE

GOD IS LOVE

Dear God, create a harmonious state
where we no longer dominate,
retaliate or exterminate.
Rise us above! Take us away!
Shield us from the pain and suffering of today.
Open up and never again close the gate.
Harvest the love and burn the hate.
Then brighten the sky seven times as bright
and be our one and only eternal light.
No! The next step is not to rise above.
It is to deepen the roots of Wisdom,
Compassion and Love.
Heaven knows, everything that has happened
up until now perfectly reflects how
mankind has walked and stalked the Earth.
Why have we allowed our belief systems
to take such a heavy toll?
Is it because we have forgotten
that we have a spiritual soul?
The position of our Soul
is neither below nor above,
it is centered in Heart
of Wisdom, Compassion and Love.
In the stillness of this center we will find
our heart, our will and our mind align.
From this harmonious space
everything falls into place.
This is the innate, loving, giving state
from which we originate.
It is who we are
and it is far from hate!
Our beliefs can be
a lock or a key
which one will they be?

Mind States

Lesser or Greater Degrees
Located on the Same Plane
  -        Neutral   +

The Closed Mind
(Negative)
I've seen that type before.
I see just what I expect to see
and the rest I make sure I ignore.

The Beginner's Mind
(Neutral)
Brand new, never seen it before,
no opinion, neither against nor for.

The Open Mind
(Positive)
It may be this or that; not or so;
ill or well, time will tell.

IN OUR HEARTS

GOD HAS SET ETERNITY

You've got to take it all in.
You've got to let it all out.
Except for the part
that is set in the heart,
and that I call
"Thou Art in Heaven,
hallowed be thy name."
You reside in every heart
as a creative, eternal flame.

LOVE IS AT THE CENTER OF OUR BEING

GOD IS LOVE

Is this not reason enough
to treat ourselves
and all living beings
with loving kindness?
If God is in me
and God is in you;
God must experience the results
of what we have chosen to do.
What type of message
would you choose to send,
if you believed that God
was on both the giving
and receiving end?

To Wisdom, what can compare?
What else can we give freely
and still have more to spare?

CARING, SHARING AND EQUALITY

Equal scales and equal measures
are one of Wisdom's greatest treasures.
"Gold there is, and rubies in abundance,
but lips that speak knowledge
are a rare…" find. (18)
Riches are to the body
what knowledge is to the mind.
Most Valuable! For knowledge
is a stepping stone to understanding,
and understanding is experienced
as a moment of truth.
Now it may be more economically profitable
to amass material wealth
than it is to accumulate wisdom
and translate it into action and words,
but unlike worldly wealth,
once we possess Wisdom
we will wisely use it
and there is no fear of losing it.
When we use our spiritual intellect,
we study, reflect and collect.
And the greater the heights we reach,
the greater is our ability
to give to others what we have to teach.
All of us have a story to tell,
a vision to see, something beneficial
to bring to our earthly community.
This is our golden opportunity
to bring about global unity,
and the first place to start
centers around our heart.
We must love money less
and adore Truth and Wisdom more!

A PIECE OF THE PUZZLE

My God, you created me.
I am a piece of your puzzle.
You are great! I am small.
I am part. You are all!

A DEDICATION

All that I say and do
is dedicated to you.
For you are my anchor;
you are the wind in my sails.
You are my success
when all else fails.
All the glory goes to you, my Lord;
all the glory goes to you!

© C. M. CROCE, 2016.

Notes

(1) Greenpeace. (2015, May 15). Seismic and sonar testing. Retrieved from http://www.greenpeace.org/usa/oceans/save-the-whales/seismic-sonar-testing/. (pg. 23 of this ms.)

(2) Von Einsiedel, O. (Director). (2014). Virunga. U.S.A.: Grain Media. (pg. 24 of this ms.)

(3) Holy Bible. (New International Version). Mark 13:14. (pg. 40 of this ms.)

(4) Meyerson, B. (2004, January 22). U.S. companies show up at conference on moving jobs overseas. The Seattle Times. Retrieved from http://old.seattletimes.com/html/businesstechnology/2001841463_outsource22.html. (pg. 54 of this ms.)

(5) Loven, J. (2004, January 21). Bush promotes job training, education in three states. Herald-Journal. p. 45. Retrieved from https://news.google.com/newspapers?nid=1876&dat=20040121&id=5DofAAAAIBAJ&sjid=adAEAAAAIBAJ&pg=5040,2626553&hl=en. (pg.54 of this ms.)

(6) Gaither, C. (2003, November 3). The white collar job migration: High-tech workers in US decry outsourcing. The Boston Globe. p. A10. (pg. 55 of this ms.)

(7) Anonymous. (1809). Works of Fisher Ames. (Boston: T.B. Wait) p. 392. (pg. 57 of this ms.)

(8) Moss, M. (2015, January 19). U.S. research lab lets livestock suffer in quest for profit. New York Times. Retrieved from http://www.nytimes.com/2015/01/20/dining/animal-welfare-at-risk-in-experiments-for-meat-industry. html?_r=0. (pg. 59 of this ms.)

(9) America's top 10 corporate tax avoiders. (2015, December 22). Retrieved from http://www.sanders.senate.gov/top-10-corporatetax-avoiders. (pg. 61 of this ms.)

(10) Huffington, A. (1999, December 8). "Leaders" are losers in battle of Seattle. Chicago Sun-Times. Retrieved from https://www.highbeam.com/doc/1P2-4524051.html.
(pg. 67 of this ms.)

(11) Prejean, H. (2005, January 13). Death in Texas. The NewYork Review of Books. Retrieved from http://www.nybooks.com/articles/2005/01/13/death-in-texas/.
(pg. 67 of this ms.)

(12) Flannery, N. P. (2012, January 19). Executive compensation:The true cost of the 10 largest CEO severance packages of the past decade. Forbes. Retrieved from http://www.forbes.com/sites/nathanielparishflannery/2012/01/19/billion-dollarblowout-top-10-largest-ceo-severance-packages-of-the-pastdecade/#3b29a33c2565. (pg. 75 of this ms.)

(13) Bump, B. (2014, May 16). GE retirees march for increase in pensions: Plan provides for no cost-of-living adjustment. The Daily Gazette. Retrieved from http://www.dailygzette.com/news/2014/may/16/. (pg. 75 of this ms.)

(14) Fabrikant, G. (2002, September 6). G.E. Expenses for ex-chief cited in divorce papers. New York Times. Retrieved from http://www.nytimes.com/2002/09/06/business/06CHIE.html?pagewanted=all.
(pg. 75 of this ms.)

(15) (2000, April 4). Electric Union News, LIX.
(pg. 76 of this ms.)

(16) (2016, February 8). Ronald Reagan quotes: Funny quotes by President Ronald Reagan. Retrieved from http://politicalhumor.about.com/quotethis/a/reaganquotes.htm.
(pg. 90 of this ms.)

(17) (2016, February 8). Hot spots. Retrieved from http://www.conservation.org/how/pages/hotspots.aspx.
(pg. 111 of this ms.)

(18) Holy Bible. (NIV). Proverbs 20:15. (pg. 130 of this ms.)

www.ingramcontent.com/pod-product-compliance
Lightning Source LLC
Chambersburg PA
CBHW070501100426
42743CB00010B/1712